Broadcast Schedule

The Origination of Something Glorious
Jesus' Birth and Beginning of Ministry
A Study of Luke 1:1–6:49

December 9, 1994–January 27, 1995

Friday	December 9	The Doctor Gives a Second Opinion Survey of Luke
Monday	December 12	The Doctor Gives a Second Opinion
Tuesday	December 13	Only the Best Luke 1:1–4
Wednesday	December 14	Only the Best
Thursday	December 15	A Baby? At Our Age? Get Serious! Luke 1:5–25
Friday	December 16	A Baby? At Our Age? Get Serious!
Monday	December 19	The Day Mary Met Gabriel Luke 1:26–56
Tuesday	December 20	The Day Mary Met Gabriel
Wednesday	December 21	The Prophet of the Most High Luke 1:57–80 .
Thursday	December 22	The Prophet of the Most High
Friday	December 23	Nativity Revisited Luke 2:1–20
Monday	December 26	Nativity Revisited
Tuesday	December 27	A Sacrifice, a Savior, a Sword Luke 2:21–38
Wednesday	December 28	A Sacrifice, a Savior, a Sword
Thursday	December 29	The Day the Pupil Stumped the Profs Luke 2:39–52
Friday	December 30	The Day the Pupil Stumped the Profs
Monday	January 2	A Study in Contrasts Luke 3
Tuesday	January 3	A Study in Contrasts

Wednesday	January 4	The Devil Never Made Him Do It Luke 4:1–13
Thursday	January 5	The Devil Never Made Him Do It
Friday	January 6	From the Frying Pan into the Fire Luke 4:14–30

Monday	January 9	From the Frying Pan into the Fire
Tuesday	January 10	Ministry at the Grassroots Level Luke 4:31–44
Wednesday	January 11	Ministry at the Grassroots Level
Thursday	January 12	What It's Like to Fish with Jesus Luke 5:1–11
Friday	January 13	What It's Like to Fish with Jesus

Monday	January 16	Great Deeds, Strong Faith . . . Big God Luke 5:12–26
Tuesday	January 17	Great Deeds, Strong Faith . . . Big God
Wednesday	January 18	Is It OK to Party with Sinners? Luke 5:27–39
Thursday	January 19	Is It OK to Party with Sinners?
Friday	January 20	The Defiant Christ Luke 6:1–11

Monday	January 23	The Defiant Christ
Tuesday	January 24	The Twelve . . . and Their Marching Orders Luke 6:12–26
Wednesday	January 25	The Twelve . . . and Their Marching Orders
Thursday	January 26	"Absurd Advice" in a Selfish Era Luke 6:27–49
Friday	January 27	"Absurd Advice" in a Selfish Era

Insight for Living • Post Office Box 69000, Anaheim, CA 92817-0900
Insight for Living Ministries • Post Office Box 2510, Vancouver, BC, Canada V6B 3W7
Insight for Living, Inc. • GPO Box 2823 EE, Melbourne, VIC 3001, Australia

Printed in the United States of America

THE ORIGINATION OF SOMETHING

Glorious

Jesus' Birth and Beginning of Ministry
A Study of Luke 1:1–6:49

BIBLE STUDY GUIDE

From the Bible-teaching ministry of

Charles R. Swindoll

INSIGHT FOR LIVING

Chuck graduated in 1963 from Dallas Theological Seminary, where he now serves as the school's fourth president, helping to prepare a new generation of men and women for the ministry. Chuck has served in pastorates in three states: Massachusetts, Texas, and California, including almost twenty-three years at the First Evangelical Free Church in Fullerton, California. His sermon messages have been aired over radio since 1979 as the *Insight for Living* broadcast. A best-selling author, Chuck has written numerous books and booklets on many subjects.

Based on the outlines and transcripts of Chuck's sermons, the study guide text is co-authored by Bryce Klabunde, a graduate of Biola University and Dallas Theological Seminary. He also wrote the Living Insights sections.

Editor in Chief:
Cynthia Swindoll

Coauthor of Text:
Bryce Klabunde

Assistant Editor:
Wendy Peterson

Copy Editors:
Deborah Gibbs
Glenda Schlahta

Editorial Assistant:
Nancy Hubbard

Text Designer:
Gary Lett

Publishing System Specialist:
Bob Haskins

Director, Communications and Marketing Division:
Deedee Snyder

Marketing Manager:
Alene Cooper

Project Coordinator:
Colette Muse

Production Manager:
John Norton

Printer:
Sinclair Printing Company

Unless otherwise identified, all Scripture references are from the New American Standard Bible, © The Lockman Foundation 1960, 1962, 1963, 1968, 1971, 1972, 1973, 1975, 1977. Used by permission. Scripture taken from the Holy Bible, New International Version © 1973, 1978, 1984 International Bible Society, used by permission of Zondervan Bible Publishers. The other translations cited are the *New Testament in Language of Today* [BECK], the *King James Version* [KJV], *The Living Bible* [LB], *The New Testament in Modern English* [PHILLIPS], and the *Revised Standard Version* [RSV]. Also cited is *The Message: The New Testament in Contemporary English* (Colorado Springs, Colo.: NavPress, 1993).

CONTENTS

INTRODUCTION

I need to begin with a confession. There are moments when I am envious of the people who lived in the days when Jesus walked the earth. If I could return to any period of time, I would return to Palestine in the first century so I could see Jesus with my own eyes. More than likely, I would have been like the people of His generation. I would probably have doubted as they doubted . . . and maybe even have said stupid things, as many of them did. But still I would love to have seen Him.

I would love to have witnessed His character, because then I would have known firsthand the character of God. I would love to have watched Him work, because then I would have seen with my own eyes the power of God. I would love to have felt His compassion, because then I would have experienced, up close and personal, the heart of God.

Philip once said, "Lord, show us the Father, and it is enough for us" (John 14:8). I'll never forget Jesus' response: "He who has seen Me has seen the Father" (v. 9).

Do you want to see God? Then study the Son of God.

In Luke's life of Christ, you'll find God to be truly real and reachable—more reachable than you may ever have known. For Luke portrays Jesus as the Son of Man, the heaven-sent Savior with a human touch.

Really, we don't have to go back in time to know Jesus. Luke has lifted Him from history and brought Him to us. Where we are. Today.

Chuck Swindoll

PUTTING TRUTH
INTO ACTION

K nowledge apart from application falls short of God's desire for
His children. He wants us to apply what we learn so that we
will change and grow. This study guide was prepared with these
goals in mind. As you go through the following pages, we hope your
desire to discover biblical truth will grow as your understanding of
God's Word increases and that you will be encouraged to apply what
you've learned.

To assist you in your study, we've included a section called
Living Insights at the end of each lesson. These exercises will
challenge you to study further and to think of specific ways to put
your discoveries into action.

On occasion a lesson is followed by a **Digging Deeper** section, which gives you additional information and resources to probe
further into some issues raised in that lesson.

There are many ways to use this guide—in personal devotions,
group studies, discussions with friends and family, and Sunday school
classes. And, of course, it's an ideal study aid when you're listening
to its corresponding *Insight for Living* radio series.

To benefit most from this study guide, we would encourage you
to consider it a spiritual journal. That's why we've included space
in the **Living Insights** for recording your thoughts and discoveries.
We hope you'll return to those sections often for review and encouragement as you continue to grow in your walk with Christ.

Bryce Klabunde

Bryce Klabunde
Co author of Text

THE ORIGINATION OF SOMETHING

Glorious

Jesus' Birth and Beginning of Ministry
A Study of Luke 1:1–6:49

LUKE: A PHYSICIAN'S OPINION

Writer: Luke, a Gentile Christian physician (first mentioned in Acts 16:10)

Date: Around A.D. 60

Style: Scholarly, detailed, people-oriented

Appeal: Directly to Greeks, but universal

Message: Jesus is truly human

Key Phrase: "The Son of Man" (Luke 19:10)

Interesting Facts:

- This is the only gospel account specifically addressed to an individual: "most excellent Theophilus" (friend of God). William Barclay calls Luke 1:1–4, "well-nigh the best Greek in the New Testament."[1]
- Luke records the first hints of Christian hymnology (1:46–55; 68–79; 2:14, 29–32).
- More pictures have been painted by artists who derive their inspiration from Luke than any other New Testament book.
- Between chapters 9 and 19 there are over 30 sayings, parables, and incidents mentioned nowhere else in Scripture.

The Son of Man . . .

. . . Announced and Appearing (About 90 percent peculiar to Luke)

Unique Introduction

"Jesus the Nazarene, who was a prophet . . . mighty in *deed* . . . and *word* in the sight of God and all the people." (24:19)

. . . Ministering and Serving

. . . Instructing and Submitting (About 60 percent peculiar to Luke)

. . . Crucified, Resurrected, and Commissioning

	1:1–4	1:5	4:13	4:14	9:50	9:51	21:38	22:1–24:53
Key Verse		"For the Son of Man has come to seek and to save that which was lost." (19:10)						
Activity		Coming			Seeking			Saving
Location		Bethlehem, Nazareth, and Judea		Galilee		Judea and Perea		Jerusalem
Time		30 years		1½ years		6 mos.	8 days	50 days

1. William Barclay, *The Gospel of Luke*, rev. ed., The Daily Study Bible Series (Philadelphia, Pa.: Westminster Press, 1975), p. 2.

Chapter 1

THE DOCTOR GIVES A
SECOND OPINION

Survey of Luke

Not long ago, a dear little woman was officially pronounced dead—which bothered her considerably, due to the fact that, despite her periodic bouts with rheumatism, she felt pretty good. Apparently, a computer operator in a Social Security office had mistakenly typed "deceased" on her account, and with a perfunctory click . . . whir . . . blip, she was gone; another casualty along the information superhighway. Eventually, she convinced the government that she was alive—only after several frustrating phone calls to workers who tended to take the word of the computer over hers![1]

How impersonal our world has become! Human life has been reduced to a number in a computer, a consumer statistic in a pollster's file, a tiny cog in a giant machine. Missing is that personal touch, that gentle look which knows our name and keeps us from getting lost in an anonymous crowd.

What we need is the presence of compassion to restore our humanity. So *who* we need is Jesus Christ.

Jesus, in the gospel of Luke especially, is shown as the compassionate Son of Man who comes "to seek and to save that which was lost" (Luke 19:10). His story, as told by Luke's pen, has been aptly described as "the gospel of the underdog."[2] Luke reveals Jesus' empathetic nature through such vignettes—which are unique to his gospel—as these:

---

1. Source unknown.

2. See William Barclay, *The Gospel of Luke*, rev. ed., The Daily Study Bible Series (Philadelphia, Pa.: Westminster Press, 1975), p. 5.

- raising to life the only son of a heartbroken widow (7:11–15)
- speaking tenderly to a nameless woman who anoints his feet with perfume (7:36–50)
- ennobling a shunned ethnic group in his parable of the good Samaritan (10:25–37)
- extending a friendly hand to a despised tax-collector (19:1–10)

"Luke," writes William Barclay, "sees no limits to the love of God."[3]

Who was this gospel writer who presents Jesus in such human and personal terms? Certainly, he must have been a caring person himself. Barclay continues,

> somehow of all the gospel writers one would have liked to meet Luke best of all, for this gentile doctor with the tremendous vision of the infinite sweep of the love of God must have been a lovely soul.[4]

Some Introductory Comments regarding Luke

Let's get acquainted with this gentle man and the gospel he wrote.

The Man and His Times

We know Luke was a doctor from Paul's passing comment in Colossians 4:14, which revealed his profession as well as Paul's feelings toward him: "Luke, the beloved physician."[5] In the Apostle's letter to Philemon, he mentioned Luke as one of his "fellow workers" (v. 24). The two men worked and traveled side by side, Paul with his lecture notes and scrolls and Luke with his medical bag and encouraging words.

From their first expedition together to Paul's final hours in a Roman dungeon, Luke remained a true friend. "Only Luke is with me," the aging Paul wrote to Timothy from his death cell (2 Tim. 4:11). Who can measure the depth of Paul's gratitude toward Luke? He

---

3. Barclay, *The Gospel of Luke*, p. 6.

4. Barclay, *The Gospel of Luke*, p. 6.

5. The context of this verse shows that Paul grouped Luke with Epaphras and Demas, distinguishing them from a previous list of Jews—"who are from the circumcision" (Col. 4:11). This leads us to believe that Luke was a Gentile. If so, he is the only Gentile writer in the New Testament.

was more than just a physician; he was a lover of people, a healer of the soul.

He was also humble. Having also authored Acts, he penned 28 percent of the New Testament,[6] more material than any other writer, and his Greek has been recognized as the finest in the Bible.[7] Yet not once did he include his own name in his work. The closest he came was in the "we" sections in Acts, in which he referred to himself in a most understated manner, beginning in 16:10:

> And when he had seen the vision, immediately we sought to go into Macedonia, concluding that God had called us to preach the gospel to them.

Apparently, this was where Luke first joined Paul's team, here in Troas, as Paul was about to embark on his journey through Macedonia. We know little about his life prior to this time. Picking up a few clues from his writing, however, some scholars have pieced together theories about his place of birth, his education, and his Christian experience.

The first clue comes from the name of the person to whom Luke addressed his gospel:

> It seemed fitting for me as well, having investigated everything carefully from the beginning, to write it out for you in consecutive order, most excellent Theophilus. (Luke 1:3)

Theophilus may have been a wealthy citizen of Antioch.[8] And since physicians were often freedmen,[9] it could be that Theophilus once owned Luke as a slave and set him free, after educating him as a physician.[10] The title, "most excellent," which Luke gives him,

---

6. John A. Martin, "Luke," in *The Bible Knowledge Commentary*, New Testament edition, ed. John F. Walvoord and Roy B. Zuck (Wheaton, Ill.: Scripture Press Publications, Victor Books, 1983), p. 199. Luke wrote more material than Paul, if we do not consider Paul as the author of Hebrews.

7. W. T. Dayton, "Luke, the gospel of," in *The Zondervan Pictorial Encyclopedia of the Bible*, ed. Merrill C. Tenney (Grand Rapids, Mich.: Zondervan Publishing House, Regency Reference Library, 1976), vol. 3, p. 1000.

8. Hayes, as quoted by Archibald Thomas Robertson in *Luke the Historian in the Light of Research* (New York, N.Y.: Charles Scribner's Sons, 1920), p. 21.

9. Ramsay, as quoted by Robertson in *Luke the Historian*, p. 19.

10. Robertson, *Luke the Historian*, p. 20.

seems to bear out that contention.

Interestingly, the name Theophilus means "friend of God." Theophilus may possibly have been a Christian, and Luke might have been the one to lead him to the Lord. Later, he decided to write the gospel and Acts to help ground his generous benefactor in the Christian faith.

Where did Luke acquire his excellent writing skills and medical training? Bible scholar A. T. Robertson provides us with a possible answer:

> If a freedman of Theophilus at Antioch, he would receive a good education in the schools there. As a physician, he would be sent by Theophilus either to Alexandria, Athens or Tarsus, the great universities of the time. Alexandria seems unlikely in the absence of any allusion to the city. We know that Luke seems familiar with Athens (Acts 17), but Tarsus is much more likely.[11]

If Luke did attend the university in Tarsus, he may have met Paul there when he was still known as Saul of Tarsus—the future Pharisee who grew up in that same city and possibly attended that same college. Another option has Paul, already a Christian before Luke started school in Tarsus, leading Luke to Christ after returning to Tarsus from Jerusalem (see Acts 9:26–30). Or, scenario number three, perhaps Luke became a Christian in Antioch after medical school. He tells us himself that

> there were some of them, men of Cyprus and Cyrene, who came to Antioch and began speaking to the Greeks also, preaching the Lord Jesus. . . . And considerable numbers were brought to the Lord. (Acts 11:20, 24b)

Luke might have been among those Greeks who "were brought to the Lord."

The exact details of his conversion remain a mystery, but we do know that Luke stuck by his commitments both to the Lord and to Paul. Robertson believes that Luke was even with Paul at his execution, and that "Luke, doubtless, saw to the burial of the body

11. Robertson, *Luke the Historian*, p. 24.

of his great friend."[12] With compassionate hands, he laid Paul to his final rest, caring for him to the very end. Truly, he was a beloved physician.

The Book and Its Themes

Every aspect of Luke's gospel exudes his personal touch, from its literary composition to its portrayal of Christ. Four characteristics of his work stand out in particular.

First, *the gospel is a sizable work, written with extreme care*. Luke wanted Theophilus and anyone else who might read his book to know the "exact truth" about Jesus' life (Luke 1:4). With the care of a physician examining a patient's charts, he not only studied the accounts of "eyewitnesses and servants of the word" (v. 2), but he also compiled reams of data and methodically recorded the events "in consecutive order" from the beginning (v. 3).

Second, *Luke is not the first gospel account*. Mark wrote the first gospel, casting Jesus in the role of a servant. Then he passed the gospel pen to Luke, who wrote his book sometime during the decade of the A.D. 50s. As a doctor, Luke gave a "second opinion" of Christ, seeing Him through the eyes of a cultured Greek as the ideal man.

Third, *Luke is a book for the detail-oriented person*. If you like knowing all the facts, you'll like Luke. Compare, for instance, the different ways Mark and Luke introduce John the Baptizer. Mark writes simply, "John the Baptist appeared in the wilderness" (1:4a). But notice the precision with which Luke, the historian, writes:

> Now in the fifteenth year of the reign of Tiberius Caesar, when Pontius Pilate was governor of Judea, and Herod was tetrarch of Galilee, and his brother Philip was tetrarch of the region of Ituraea and Trachonitis, and Lysanias was tetrach of Abilene, in the high priesthood of Annas and Caiaphas, the word of God came to John, the son of Zacharias, in the wilderness. (Luke 3:1–2)

Luke scatters historical gems like these throughout his book. He also places here and there other little treasures: medical terms, nautical facts, and details about Jesus' life not mentioned in the other gospels.

---

12. Robertson, *Luke the Historian*, p. 29.

Fourth, *Luke highlights the humanity of Jesus*. It makes sense that, of the gospel writers, the physician would be the one most interested in the man Jesus. Reading Luke, you get the feeling you are listening through the doctor's stethoscope to the heartbeat of our Lord, feeling His empathy as He reaches out to those who cross His path. Let's examine a few of the events in Jesus' life that are unique to Luke's account and that particularly draw out Jesus' humanity.

Several Significant Scenes Unique to Luke

Between chapters 9 and 19 alone, J. Sidlow Baxter counts "no less than thirty or more" scenes exclusive to Luke.[13] Then he observes,

> It is not only the intrinsic worth of these parables, miracles, incidents, which makes them mean so much to us: it is the way they reveal *HIM*. One after another they come, like so many successive floodlights of different colour turned on an object of supreme attractiveness. . . . All bear on the *human nature* of our Lord.[14]

These "successive floodlights" shine on every area of Christ's life, from His birth to His death, resurrection, and ascension.

Luke Describes Jesus' Birth and Childhood

Luke's is the most intimate account of Jesus' birth. Where Matthew takes a snapshot of the event — "Jesus was born in Bethlehem of Judea in the days of Herod the king" (Matt. 2:1a)— Luke films the drama in Technicolor. As we read his account, we get to walk beside the weary couple to Bethlehem while Mary "is with child" (Luke 2:5b), feel the disappointment of the closed inn, watch with wonder at the birth, see the loving mother wrap the Child in cloths and lay Him in the manger (v. 7). We fall before the angels, search with the shepherds, join in the adoration, and gaze at young Mary as she caresses the Baby, treasuring this eternal moment (vv. 8–20).

Luke keeps the cameras rolling through Jesus' childhood. We go with the family to Jesus' dedication in the temple (vv. 22–24); we hear the blessings and return to his Nazareth home (vv. 25–39).

13. J. Sidlow Baxter, "The Gospel according to Luke," in *Explore the Book* (Grand Rapids, Mich.: Zondervan Publishing House, Academie Books, 1960), p. 234.

14. Baxter, "The Gospel according to Luke," p. 235.

Then we get a glimpse of the boy Jesus as a twelve-year-old in the temple, amazing the elders and already attending to His Father's business (vv. 41–49).

Luke Traces Jesus' Genealogy Back to Adam

Matthew traces Jesus' lineage to Abraham because he wants to display Jesus to the Jews as the Hebrew Messiah. Mark considers a genealogy unnecessary for his purposes and leaves it out. John uses a prologue instead of a genealogy to establish his theme of Jesus' deity. Luke's approach is different still: focusing on Jesus' humanity, he links Jesus to Adam, the first human!

Luke Devotes Much Space to and Interest in People

A child of Adam like everybody else, Luke's Jesus is a Savior for all people, regardless of race, sex, or creed, irrespective of social status, physical health, or moral background. That's why Luke includes unique stories that illustrate Jesus' compassion for everyone: the hemorrhaging woman who "could not be healed by anyone" (8:43–48), the parable of the prodigal son (15:11–32), the ten lepers (17:11–19).

Luke Describes the Suffering and Death of Jesus in Graphic Detail

As vivid as Luke's account was of Jesus' birth, it pales in the light of his graphic portrayal of Jesus' death. Using his palette of medical terms, he paints a striking picture of Jesus' suffering. Viewing Luke's Passion account will truly make you feel as if you were there when they crucified our Lord.

Luke Provides Us with Two "Hidden Outlines" of His Book

Luke's theme verse also reveals a memorable outline for his gospel:

> "For the Son of Man has come to seek and to save
> that which was lost." (19:10)

From the Nativity through Jesus' wilderness temptation (1:1–4:13), the Son of Man *comes*; from Jesus' first public appearance to His ministry in Galilee and final trip to Jerusalem (4:14–21:38), the Son of Man *seeks*; and from the Last Supper through His post-resurrection appearances (chaps. 22–24), the Son of Man *saves*.

7

Another outline emerges from the conversation Jesus had with the two men on the road to Emmaus. He asks them what they're talking about, and they respond:

> "The things about Jesus the Nazarene, who was a prophet mighty in deed and word in the sight of God and all the people, and how the chief priests and our rulers delivered Him up to the sentence of death, and crucified Him. But we were hoping that it was He who was going to redeem Israel. Indeed, besides all this, it is the third day since these things happened. But also some women among us amazed us. When they were at the tomb early in the morning, and did not find His body, they came, saying that they had also seen a vision of angels, who said that He was alive." (24:19b–23)

Their response to Him hands us the book of Luke in a nutshell:

- Jesus appears as the promised Prophet (1:1–4:13)

- Jesus shows himself to be "mighty in deed" during His Galilee ministry (4:14–9:50)

- Journeying toward Jerusalem, Jesus becomes "mighty in word" (9:51–21:38)

- In Jerusalem, Jesus is crucified and resurrected (chaps. 22–24)

The Value of Seeing Christ as the Son of Man

If you sometimes feel lost in a world that degrades and dehumanizes, allow the ancient physician to acquaint you with the Son of Man—the divine One with the human touch.

He identifies with the real world. Jesus knows where we live and work. He toiled under the harsh sun and felt the hard earth under His feet. He understands what real life is all about.

He is touched with real needs. We might see Jesus as deity, standing in raiment of shimmering white; but we also need to see Jesus as the Son of Man, kneeling beside a ragged leper. As the Son of Man, He views our human suffering through the eyes of One who suffered Himself. As the Son of Man, He feels our pain as if it were His own.

He brings real comfort. Knowing that someone understands is reassuring, but Jesus takes us even further. He offers us real comfort as the Great Physician who not only sympathizes with souls lost in sin but saves them through the power of the Cross.

Living Insights

Commentator J. Sidlow Baxter sheds light on one of the purposes for Luke's emphasis on Jesus as the Son of Man.

> We think of Luke as a Greek writing to a Greek. The Greeks were an idealistic-minded people. Their philosophers and moralists had their theoretic ideal of perfect manhood. Luke sets forth Jesus in all the simple purity, lovely naturalness, profound beauty, and moral sublimity of His sinless manhood. . . . To Christian believers, however, Jesus means something nearer than that: He is our perfect *example*. His manhood is our *pattern*. We are called to live *like* Him.[15]

To be like Jesus . . . that is our life's aim and the reason for this study. Our desire is not necessarily that you remember every date and outline, but that you take a good, long look at Jesus. Listen to His heartbeat as Luke did when he wrote his gospel. Feel Jesus' passions, and experience His joys and sorrows. Let His attitudes be your attitudes; His actions, your actions.

As you set out on this great adventure of Christlikeness, take these words as your guiding compass:

> Whoever claims to live in him must walk as Jesus did. (1 John 2:6 NIV)

Living Insights

In this Living Insight, let's put the principle of Christlikeness into action right away. Of the many magnificent themes that tower like trees within Luke's gospel, the giant redwood, according to

---

15. Baxter, "The Gospel according to Luke," p. 263.

William Barclay, is this: "Jesus Christ is for all [people] without distinction."[16] Let's use the following categories to acquaint ourselves a little better with Luke's book and get a feel for this great theme. Look up the verses, and jot down the ways in which Jesus expresses His love and concern for all people.

The Samaritans

9:51–56 _____

10:30–37 _____

The Gentiles

4:25–27 _____

7:6–10 _____

The Poor

16:19–31 _____

21:1–4 _____

The Outcasts and Sinners

7:36–50 _____

19:1–10 _____

23:39–43 _____

As you prepare to meet this Jesus who came for *all* people, ask yourself, "What is my attitude toward outsiders?" Are there certain groups or types of people you find difficult to love? Explain.

_____

_____

_____

Commit yourself right now to let Christ's compassion for the lost of this world fill your heart. May the wellspring of your love for others grow deeper with each page of His life that you read.

16. Barclay, *The Gospel of Luke*, p. 5.

Chapter 2

ONLY THE BEST

Luke 1:1–4

What if Luke had written his gospel in today's market-driven world? We can imagine the letter some high-powered publisher might have sent him.

> Dear Dr. Luke:
>
> I anticipate big things from your book on the life of Christ—big, *big*, BIG! I see Christmas sales going through the roof! But, Luke, if I'm going to ship product by September, I need chapters coming in. How about 1 through 5 . . . tomorrow. Just kidding! ASAP, OK? You're a champ!
>
> Of course, I appreciate your desire to investigate your sources thoroughly, but you must understand my time constraints. If we miss Christmas, our profits will be cut, *cut*, CUT! Is there any way you can round a few corners in the research department? Maybe drop some details? Trim a few obscure stories? I can move a shorter book just as well, and no one will know the difference.
>
> Respectfully yours,
> Pete "Print-It" Jones, Editor

Thankfully, Luke didn't have to contend with this sort of pressure. He had the freedom to study his sources thoroughly, to plan his themes and craft his words to bring out the grandeur of Christ. As a result, like the ancient pyramids, his well-constructed book has defied the winds of time. And, because it was built with excellence, his gospel will continue to stand firm.

In contrast, our world seems to thrive on mediocrity. In many places, a just-get-by mentality has replaced the drive to do one's best. Getting the job done seems to be valued higher than doing a good job.

As Christians, we can get sucked into this whirlpool way of thinking, losing sight of why God wants us to strive for excellence. So, before turning to Luke, let's examine what God has to say about His standard for us.

A Standard That Cannot Be Ignored

Paul's letter to the Colossians provides a solid scriptural basis for pursuing excellence.

Scriptural Basis

In chapter 3, Paul shows us two sets of targets toward which we can aim our lives. The first list of ideals is for the individual; the second, for home and work.

For the individual, excellence in character and in relationships is measured by

> a heart of compassion, kindness, humility, gentleness and patience; bearing with one another, and forgiving each other, whoever has a complaint against anyone; just as the Lord forgave you, so also should you. And beyond all these things put on love, which is the perfect bond of unity. (vv. 12–14)

According to verse 15, "the peace of Christ" rules an excellent heart. And, according to verse 16, an excellent attitude dwells within a person who is praising and thanking God.

To sum up his thoughts, Paul broadens his scope to include the entire landscape of our thoughts and actions:

> And whatever you do in word or deed, do all in the name of the Lord Jesus, giving thanks through Him to God the Father. (v. 17)

His second list addresses the various roles we fulfill in the home and at work and the excellence to which we can aspire:

Roles	Excellence to Be Expressed
Wives	"Be subject to your husbands" (v. 18)
Husbands	"Love your wives" (v. 19)
Children	"Be obedient to your parents" (v. 20)
Fathers	"Do not exasperate your children" (v. 21)
Slaves (employees)	"Obey those who are your masters . . . with sincerity of heart" (v. 22)
Masters (employers)	"Grant to your slaves justice and fairness" (4:1)

He bundles this group of concepts with the same ribbon of thought we saw in 3:17:

> Whatever you do, do your work heartily, as for the
> Lord rather than for men. (v. 23)

"Whatever you do"—whether it's teaching a Sunday school class, nurturing your child, writing a report, or plowing a field—do it *heartily*. The word in Greek literally means "from the soul." Phillips translates the phrase: "put your whole heart and soul into it."

Why? Because, ultimately, we work for the Lord, not for people. And, according to verse 24, one day He will reward us for our seen and unseen labors:

> Knowing that from the Lord you will receive the
> reward of the inheritance. It is the Lord Christ
> whom you serve. (v. 24)

Practical Excellence

What would it be like if we did everything "heartily, as for the Lord"? No longer would we do things "just to get by." We'd aim to become all God created us to be; we'd work to our fullest abilities . . . because Christ deserves our very best.

Luke composed his gospel with this desire to give his best to the Lord. He put his heart and soul into his work, and it shows in the level of excellence on every page.

A Statement of Luke's Precision

The first four verses of Luke are like a clear spring of excellence that bubbles into the sparkling river that forms the rest of his gospel. According to William Barclay, these lines represent "the best bit of Greek in the New Testament."

> Luke uses here the very form of introduction which
> the great Greek historians all used. . . .
> It is as if Luke said to himself, "I am writing the
> greatest story in the world and nothing but the best
> is good enough for it."[1]

1. William Barclay, *The Gospel of Luke*, rev. ed., The Daily Study Bible Series (Philadelphia, Pa.: Westminster Press, 1975), p. 7.

Let's examine four ways Luke made his gospel the best it could be.

He Applied Excellence in His Research

Being a good historian, Luke took the research side of his task seriously. Having not been with Christ personally, he followed two avenues to the information he needed. He names his sources in chapter 1, verses 1–2:

> Inasmuch as many have undertaken to compile an account of the things accomplished among us, just as those who from the beginning were eyewitnesses and servants of the word have handed them down to us.

We get our word *autopsy* from the Greek word for *eyewitnesses*, which literally means "seeing with one's own eyes."[2] These eyewitnesses weren't simply casual observers; they were discerning examiners. They watched Jesus at the peak of His popularity and during the depths of His agony. With their own eyes they observed Him giving sight to the blind, strength to the lame, and life to the dead. They were reliable witnesses.

Luke also depended on the "servants of the word" for information—people who kept records of Jesus' life. Certainly, the gospel writer John Mark was among this group, as well as some of the apostles. They knew the facts and passed them down until they finally fell into the hands of Luke.

Digging up data was only the beginning of Luke's task. With the skill of a gemologist, Luke had to carefully study the information to know which light and angle he should use to most accurately reveal Christ's radiant nature.

He Employed Excellence in Interpretation of the Facts

Luke recounted his method of interpretation in verse 3, "It seemed fitting for me as well, having investigated everything carefully from the beginning." Although others had already written about Christ, he believed that he could make a significant contribution to the subject as well. But he had to be careful not to let his own opinions get in the way of the truth. Statesman Bernard Baruch once observed,

---

2. *Merriam-Webster's Collegiate Dictionary*, 10th ed., see "autopsy."

Every man has a right to his own opinion, but no man has a right to be wrong in his facts.[3]

To ensure accuracy, Luke *investigated* everything. In Greek, the word means "to follow along a thing in mind, to trace carefully."[4] He left no stone unturned as he followed the trail of information about Christ's life from beginning to end.

He Communicated Excellence in His Writing

With the groundwork completed, Luke was ready to put pen to paper and construct his gospel—"in consecutive order" (v. 3b). In some places, that means he wrote chronologically; in others, topically; and in still others, geographically. In each method, he built his life of Christ in an orderly manner—not by slapping together two-by-fours but by carefully mortising themes and events to make a structure worthy of Christ.

As a communicator, Luke inspires all who teach or write to be diligent in their craft. We never reach a place where we can be slipshod about the facts or negligent about studying and crediting sources. People guide their lives according to our teaching. Don't they deserve our best? Doesn't Christ deserve our best?

He Demonstrated Excellence in His Concern

Last, Luke shows excellence through his driving concern that his friend and possible former master, Theophilus, receive a firm theological footing. Addressing him, Luke says he wrote his gospel "so that you might know the exact truth about the things you have been taught" (v. 4).

It's one thing to help deliver a newborn Christian into God's family, but it's another thing entirely to safely bring up that baby believer in the Lord. In Luke's day, false teachers roamed the cities like bandits, stealing away defenseless minds. "Feel-good" religious clichés wouldn't be strong enough to safeguard Theophilus; so Luke set out to surround him with rock-solid truth, providing him a sheltered place in which to grow.

---

3. Bernard Baruch, as quoted by Haddon W. Robinson in *Biblical Preaching* (Grand Rapids, Mich.: Baker Book House, 1980), p. 142.

4. Archibald Thomas Robertson, *Word Pictures in the New Testament* (Grand Rapids, Mich.: Baker Book House, 1930), vol. 2, p. 6.

The Challenge to Give "Only the Best"

A mediocre job may be good enough to meet the world's standards, but we don't serve the world. We serve the Lord Jesus Christ. Let that fact inspire you to excellence. Musicians, play your instruments for Him. Architects, design your buildings for Him. Homemakers, nurture your families for Him. Your work is an extension of yourself—and of He who lives in you; let it be an expression of heartfelt praise to the One who gave His best for us and who deserves our best in return.

 *Living Insights*   STUDY ONE

For centuries, admirers have been astounded at Leonardo da Vinci's remarkable attention to detail in his masterpiece *The Last Supper*. Each brushstroke contributes to the drama on canvas, from the items on the table to the lines on the walls to the anguished faces of the disciples—who ask, "Surely not I, Lord?" (Matt. 26:22).

With this same attention to detail and passion for beauty, Luke composes his mural of Christ's life. It is the small things, in Luke's gospel as in da Vinci's painting, that make for excellent works of art.

Although you may not be an artist, paying attention to details is an important part of striving for excellence. It is fitting that Luke is the one who records this teaching of Jesus:

> "He who is faithful in a very little thing is faithful also
> in much; and he who is unrighteous in a very little
> thing is unrighteous also in much." (Luke 16:10)

In life's busyness, have you left behind a trail of little things still undone? Perhaps it's time to slow down a bit so you can take care of the details. You are God's masterpiece in the making; let Him concentrate on the small things that can contribute so much to the quality of the finished product.

 Living Insights   STUDY TWO

Of the many statements in the New Testament that define Christ's divine nature, few glisten with as much splendor as the following one in Hebrews 1:3–4.

And He is the radiance of His glory and the exact representation of His nature, and upholds all things by the word of His power. When He had made purification of sins, He sat down at the right hand of the Majesty on high; having become as much better than the angels, as He has inherited a more excellent name than they.

Resident within Christ's name is all of His magnificent glory. The writer contends that His name is more excellent than even that of the angels who adorn the throne room of God. It is higher and greater than any other—

At the name of Jesus every knee should bow, of those who are in heaven, and on earth, and under the earth. (Phil. 2:10)

Here is an amazing thought: Everything we do is to be done in the *name* of Jesus (Col. 3:17)!

We are to emblazon the name Jesus Christ across our work, our relationships, and our character. How proud would Christ be to have His name on these areas of your life?

Your work: _____

_____

Your relationships: _____

_____

Your character: _____

_____

Do you need to make any changes so that you better represent Christ's glory to those around you? If so, in what ways can you display His excellence in all that you do?

_____

_____

_____

_____

Chapter 3

A BABY? AT OUR AGE? GET SERIOUS!

Luke 1:5–25

God is full of surprises! When we expect His pitch to come low and inside, it sails high and outside. When we look for Him at the front door, He enters by the back door. When we think He's surely going to jump into action, He holds back—like Jesus did when Lazarus lay dying. And about the time we give up hope, He comes out of nowhere with life in His hands.

God has a history of pulling off surprises. The Red Sea must have looked like the end of the road for the newly freed Hebrew nation . . . then, surprise! God parted the waters. The walls of Jericho must have towered ominously over Joshua and his army. Surprise! One shout and they fell down flat. The starving widow of Zarephath must have thought her life was over when she went to scrape her last meal out of the bowl of flour and jar of oil. Surprise! "The bowl of flour was not exhausted nor did the jar of oil become empty, according to the word of the Lord" (1 Kings 17:16a).

We can't count God out of any situation, because, as Jesus said, "With God all things are possible" (Matt. 19:26b; see also Luke 1:37). He is omnipotent, infinite, unrestricted, and self-sufficient. Those attributes boggle our minds, because we are just the opposite— impotent, finite, limited, and needy. Unlike us, He feels no frustrations, faces no barriers, entertains no fears. To God, what we call impossible is no big deal!

Consider Zacharias and Elizabeth, who had resigned themselves to a childless home. After all, it was impossible for Elizabeth to get pregnant at her age . . . right?

Surprise!

A Case in Point: Zacharias and Elizabeth

The Lord unveiled His surprise for this couple at a momentous time in history. The dawn of His messianic promise for the Jews was just about to stretch its golden rays across the land. According to commentator David Gooding,

The night had been long and, for Israel, at times very dark. But through it all—through times of national success and disaster, through the conquest and the monarchy, through the exile and return—hope had persisted that the night would at last end and, as Malachi put it, "the sun of righteousness would arise with healing in his wings" (4:2).[1]

That secret hope still burned—but dimly—under Herod's despotic rule. Herod murdered any who might pose a threat to his reign as king of the Jews; he would be the one who would issue the barbarous order to kill all the male babies in Bethlehem (Matt. 2:16). Such darkness! How the righteous strained to see the harbinger of dawn the prophets had spoken of. Gooding continues:

> Isaiah had prophesied (40:3–8) that before the "glory of the Lord" should "be revealed," a forerunner would be sent to prepare the way of the Lord. Malachi had added that before the day of the Lord came, the prophet Elijah would be sent to "turn the hearts of the fathers to the children and the hearts of the children to their fathers . . ." (4:5–6). And now more than four hundred years after Malachi the seemingly interminable night was coming to its end: the dawn was about to break.[2]

The Couple in the Spotlight

At that dramatic moment, without notice, God slipped into the world and selected an ordinary priest and his wife. Concerning their character, Luke says,

> And they were both righteous in the sight of God, walking blamelessly in all the commandments and requirements of the Lord. (Luke 1:6)

And yet this godly pair "had no child, because Elizabeth was barren, and they were both advanced in years" (v. 7).

No little one's playful splash of laughter filled their home.

---

1. David Gooding, *According to Luke: A New Exposition of the Third Gospel* (Grand Rapids, Mich.: William B. Eerdmans Publishing Co., 1987), p. 33.

2. Gooding, *According to Luke*, pp. 33–34.

No parental pride swelled their hearts with joy. Only emptiness. Barrenness. Any involuntarily childless couple can understand Zacharias and Elizabeth's silent sorrow as time slowly erased their hopes of pregnancy. To make matters worse, a social and spiritual stigma was attached to childlessness in those days. According to William Barclay,

> The Jewish Rabbis said that seven people were excommunicated from God and the list began, "A Jew who has no wife, or a Jew who has a wife and who has no child." Childlessness was a valid ground for divorce.[3]

Shadowing Zacharias and Elizabeth were the bleak clouds of sorrow and shame. Who would ever imagine that in this aging, heartbroken couple God would plant the seed of hope for the world? But He did!

The Angelic Visit and Announcement

And this is what happened.

> Now it came about, while [Zacharias] was performing his priestly service before God in the appointed order of his division, according to the custom of the priestly office, he was chosen by lot to enter the temple of the Lord and burn incense. (vv. 8-9)

In Zacharias' time, the priesthood bulged with more than twenty thousand members divided into twenty-four divisions, and "each division was on duty twice a year, for a week on each occasion."[4] During one of Zacharias' weeks of temple duty, he, by "chance," was chosen to burn the incense.

> To be the offering priest was an honour which some priests never received and none were permitted more than once. As the sacrificed animal burned outside, the offering priest poured incense over a live coal

---

3. William Barclay, *The Gospel of Luke*, rev. ed., The Daily Study Bible Series (Philadelphia, Pa.: Westminster Press, 1975), p. 10.

4. Leon Morris, *The Gospel according to St. Luke*, The Tyndale New Testament Commentary series (Grand Rapids, Mich.: William B. Eerdmans Publishing Co., 1974), p. 68.

on the altar within the Holy Place. As the smoke arose, he prayed some set prayer for the blessing, peace, and messianic redemption of Israel.[5]

Zacharias had looked forward to this moment his entire life. All alone in the sacred chamber, he carefully observed each step of the liturgy, while "the whole multitude of the people were in prayer outside" (v. 10).

Inside, as Zacharias approached the altar, waves of heat rose from the glowing embers. Impassioned prayers flowed out of his priestly soul—prayers for his people, prayers for himself. With one motion, he lifted the censer and let its contents spill over the coals, enveloping him and his petitions in a billowing, ambrosial cloud.

Suddenly, through the mist,

> an angel of the Lord appeared to him, standing to the right of the altar of incense. (v. 11)

Zacharias' face paled; his knees went weak; his heart pounded. According to Luke, he "was troubled when he saw him, and fear gripped him" (v. 12). But the angel loosened fear's hold on Zacharias with these words of comfort:

> "Do not be afraid, Zacharias, for your petition has been heard, and your wife Elizabeth will bear you a son, and you will give him the name John. And you will have joy and gladness, and many will rejoice at his birth." (vv. 13–14)

Not only will Zacharias' prayer for himself and his wife be answered, but his petition for the nation will be granted too. For his son—*his* son—"will be great in the sight of the Lord," the angel said,

> and he will drink no wine or liquor; and he will be filled with the Holy Spirit, while yet in his mother's womb. And he will turn back many of the sons of Israel to the Lord their God. And it is he who will go as a forerunner before Him in the spirit and power of Elijah, to turn the hearts of the fathers back to

5. E. Earle Ellis, *The Gospel of Luke*, rev. ed., New Century Bible Commentary series (1974; reprint, Grand Rapids, Mich.: William B. Eerdmans Publishing Co., 1983), p. 68.

the children, and the disobedient to the attitude of the righteous; so as to make ready a people prepared for the Lord." (vv. 15–17)

Malachi's prophecy will come true—the messianic sun will rise on Israel after all. And the one to prepare the nation to greet the dawn will be the son of Zacharias . . . *surprise*, Zacharias!

Zacharias?

Tripping in unbelief over the hem of the angel's message, the priest couldn't get past these words: "Elizabeth will bear you a son." How can *Elizabeth* have a baby? How can *he* be the father?

> And Zacharias said to the angel, "How shall I know this for certain? For I am an old man, and my wife is advanced in years." (v. 18)

Like us sometimes, Zacharias was living in the backwash of his own limitations, and he couldn't foresee the marvels that God wanted to do for him if he only believed. Using the emphatic first person in Greek, *ego*, Luke boldfaces Zacharias' doubt—"For *I* am an old man." But, employing the same word, *ego*, the angel silences the old man's excuse . . . and his tongue.

> "I am Gabriel, who stands in the presence of God; and I have been sent to speak to you, and to bring you this good news. And behold, you shall be silent and unable to speak until the day when these things take place, because you did not believe my words, which shall be fulfilled in their proper time." (vv. 19–20, emphasis added)

Zacharias received a sign, all right—but not the kind he expected. His words of unbelief would stick in his throat, until the day he would name his newborn son.

The Result of God's Intervention

Can you imagine Zacharias' frustration when he finally left Gabriel's presence? As a priest, he had been God's spokesman his entire life; now he had a scoop on the most exciting news from heaven to hit Israel in four hundred years, and he couldn't make a sound about it!

Meanwhile, the people outside had been wondering why he was taking so long in the temple (v. 21), but when he finally came out and couldn't speak to them,

> they realized that he had seen a vision in the temple;
> and he kept making signs to them, and remained
> mute. (v. 22b)

After he returned home, Elizabeth became pregnant, just as Gabriel had said she would (vv. 23–24). Her initial response to God's surprise was different from her husband's. She rejoiced!

> "This is the way the Lord has dealt with me in the
> days when He looked with favor upon me, to take
> away my disgrace among men." (v. 25)

Things to Remember When God Steps In

Today, if we think God has run out of surprises, we could be in for the surprise of our lives! When it comes to understanding the ways God works, Zacharias and Elizabeth's story teaches three principles.

First, *our impossibilities are the platforms upon which God does His best work*. Have you begun to lose hope that a certain family member will change his or her ways? If you're unemployed, do you sometimes wonder whether you will ever find a job? Remember, nothing frustrates God. When the night looks the bleakest, He does His best work. It may take time, though, so we must also remember this next principle.

Second, *God's delays are not necessarily His denials*. God's, "Wait" does not necessarily imply, "No." He may simply be saying, "Not right now." So, rather than letting His delays cause doubt, let them cause growth in your life. During the wait, experience to the fullest what trusting Christ really means.

Third, *when God intervenes, His surprises are always for His immediate glory and for our ultimate good*. Like Zacharias, you may pray a long time for something only to have God answer your prayers in an unusual and unexpected way. How would you react? Would you doubt His ability to do the impossible after so many years of waiting? Instead, be like Elizabeth, who accepted God's gift graciously, even though it came later than she hoped. It may be a surprise to you, but to God, it's just a part of His sovereign plan.

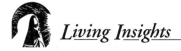 *Living Insights*

Every woman, according to Dr. David Reuben, carries within her body a vast potential for life.

> At birth each ovary contains hundreds of thousands of immature eggs, many of which will degenerate before puberty. During the average woman's life only about 400 will be released, and only two will be fertilized. So that's a reserve of tens of thousands of eggs.[6]

So much potential, yet so few of her eggs bear fruit. For the childless woman who longs to have a baby, the fruit may never appear. And as each bud on her biological tree dies, her dreams die, one by one—until, finally, the last bud withers, and she is barren forever. Gone is any hope of pregnancy. Gone is any vision of cradling a newborn to her breast . . . holding her baby's fingers . . . playing patty-cake . . . nurturing the image of her love to maturity.

For Elizabeth, each fruitless month that passed must have ripped a little of hope's fabric from her heart. "Maybe next month," she would reassure herself, but as the months turned to years, her hopes must have turned threadbare and worn. Finally, one day, she saw in her reflection the wrinkles in her skin and the age of her body, and she knew her time had passed. How her tears must have flowed. How deep her sorrow must have been as her frayed dreams scattered in the wind.

Salt for her wounded heart was the nagging question *why?* During Elizabeth's day, it was held that children were God's gift to those who served Him well.

> Behold, children are a gift of the Lord;
> The fruit of the womb is a reward. (Ps. 127:3)

According to Luke, she and her husband walked "blamelessly in all the commandments and requirements of the Lord" (Luke 1:6b). So why did God withhold the reward? Was there some sin she hadn't atoned for? Was there some law she hadn't kept? Was there something wrong with her?

---

6. David Reuben, M.D., "The Body Quiz," *Reader's Digest*, April 1994, p. 142.

Have you asked yourself those kinds of questions when your dreams go unfulfilled? Do you blame yourself? Do you feel that God has forgotten you?

Remember, *God's delays are not necessarily His denials*. Elizabeth's reward came later in life. God may do the same for you, or He may reserve your reward for heaven. Are you willing to keep waiting and trusting?

That's not an easy question to answer, particularly if you are facing the kind of disappointment Elizabeth faced. We've provided you some space to work out your own answer before the Lord. Describe your impossible situation to Him and your feelings of loss. Express to Him as much faith as you can, then allow Him some room to give you what you need to restore your hope.

Living Insights

Did God really part the Red Sea? Did the Hebrews really shout down the mighty walls of Jericho? Did the widow's bowl of flour and jar of oil really replenish themselves?

At one time or another, we all have probably wondered about God's capacity to do the impossible. Doubting is a natural part of our human nature. Zacharias had trouble believing in God's supernatural ability, and he was talking to an angel!

Even Zacharias' son, John, wrestled with doubt when he was thrown into an impossible situation—prison. Take a moment to read the account in Matthew 11:2–6.

Why do you think John might have questioned Jesus' messianic claim?

How did Jesus reassure John that He was who He said He was (see vv. 4–5)?

_____

_____

Write your own list of amazing things you've seen Christ do. You might list some names of people whose lives He has changed or some circumstances in which you've seen Him work mightily.

_____

_____

_____

_____

_____

_____

_____

Keep this list in your mind when doubt imprisons your faith. And don't be afraid to bring your questions to the Lord as John did. He's more than willing to remind you that He really can do the impossible.

Chapter 4

THE DAY MARY
MET GABRIEL

Luke 1:26–56

From the home of Zacharias and Elizabeth in mountainous Judea, Luke shifts the scene to the rolling hills of Galilee, to a teenage girl dreaming about her future. Her life just starting to bloom, Mary peers into the coming years with hopeful eyes. How will God use her? Whom will she marry? When will she have a family of her own?

One day, her parents unveil their plans for her to marry Joseph, the carpenter. Mary's mind whirls as she absorbs this news and tries to picture herself as Joseph's wife. John Wood explores her inner thoughts:

> By night, she imagines how she will arrange her furniture and decorate her room. How fortunate that Joseph is a carpenter and can make what they cannot afford to buy. By day, with needle and thread, she works her dreams into linen. And when she dreams again, it is of children. "Lord, make me fruitful as Leah but beloved as Rachel. Let me live to see my children's children."[1]

But never in her wildest imaginings does she foresee the Child God has in her future. Life's ordinary things fill her mind now—a husband, a home, a family. Then she comes face-to-face with an angel, and all at once, everything is changed.

A Visit That Would Change Everything

Mary meets the same angel Zacharias encountered in the temple. However, no burning coals and sacred altar surround Gabriel's appearance this time. Instead, he comes without ceremony to the humblest of villages.

---

1. John Wood, "The Trouble with God's Favor," *Ministry RTS* (Jackson, Miss.: Reformed Theological Seminary), Winter 1991, p. 8.

Mary and Gabriel

According to Luke, God sent Gabriel to Nazareth during "the sixth month" of Elizabeth's pregnancy. Nazareth was a trifling town located just off the main trade routes (Luke 1:26). Some have thought the city housed a troop of Roman soldiers. Certainly, its moral reputation was less than shining among the Judean Jewry. Nathanael voiced the popular sentiment toward the city and its surly citizens: "Can any good thing come out of Nazareth?" (John 1:46).

"Yes!" answers the One who sees the goodness in the heart. For in Nazareth, there lived

> a virgin engaged to a man whose name was Joseph, of the descendants of David; and the virgin's name was Mary. (Luke 1:27)

Twice in this verse, Luke refers to Mary as a virgin, *parthenos* in Greek, which in this context means "one who had not yet had sexual relations."[2] Jim Bishop, in *The Day Christ Was Born*, reveals its importance in the Jewish betrothal customs of that day.

> When the two mothers and two fathers were agreed, the *qiddushin* took place. This is a formal betrothal, and much more binding than any other. The *qiddushin* has the finality of marriage. Once the marriage contract was negotiated, even though the marriage ceremony had not occurred, the bridegroom-to-be could not be rid of his betrothed except through divorce. . . .
>
> If Joseph had died between *qiddushin* and marriage, Mary would have been his legal widow. If, in the same period, another man had had knowledge of her, Mary would have been punished as an adulteress.[3]

During her engagement, Mary's purity was under scrutiny. God, however, chooses this time to send Gabriel with some wonderful yet unsettling news.

---

2. Walter L. Liefeld, "Luke," in *The Expositor's Bible Commentary*, ed. Frank E. Gaebelein (Grand Rapids, Mich.: Zondervan Publishing House, Regency Reference Library, 1984), vol. 8, p. 830.

3. Jim Bishop, *The Day Christ Was Born* (San Francisco, Calif.: HarperCollins Publishers, HarperSanFrancisco, 1978), pp. 29–30.

And coming in, he said to her, "Hail, favored one! The Lord is with you." (v. 28)

Mighty Gabriel deals gently with Mary, who is, remember, just a young teenager, perhaps between thirteen and fifteen years old. He calls her "favored one"; the old Latin version reads *gratiae plena*, "full of grace." As one commentator puts it, the angel is saying, "'You are full of grace which you have received . . . you are in a unique sense a divinely favored person.'"[4] God has chosen her above all other women to receive this gift, and the angel marvels at God's grace on her life. But Mary has no idea why he has appeared to her, so she becomes "greatly troubled at this statement" (v. 29). Quickly, Gabriel continues:

> "Do not be afraid, Mary; for you have found favor with God. And behold, you will conceive in your womb, and bear a son, and you shall name Him Jesus. He will be great, and will be called the Son of the Most High; and the Lord God will give Him the throne of His father David; and He will reign over the house of Jacob forever; and His kingdom will have no end." (vv. 30–33)

For generations, Mary's people have anxiously waited for the Great Deliverer Gabriel describes. Devout ones have searched the prophecies for clues about Him. Fathers have taught their families to watch for Him. Mothers have peered into the eyes of their newborns, wondering whether their child might be the One. And now God, in His infinite wisdom, has said, "Enough waiting! The Messiah will come now, through the womb of a virgin."

That last part is what furrows Mary's brow. Not yet married, she timidly asks Gabriel, "How can this be, since I am a virgin?"— literally, "since I have known no man?" (v. 34).

Zacharias, in unbelief, requested a sign. Mary, however, doesn't ask for proof; she simply wonders about the process. How can a virgin have a baby? So the angel graciously explains:

> "The Holy Spirit will come upon you, and the power

---

4. William Hendriksen, *Exposition of the Gospel according to Luke*, New Testament Commentary series (Grand Rapids, Mich.: Baker Book House, 1978), p. 85. Hendriksen adds, "It is wrongly interpreted as if it meant, 'Mary, you are filled with grace which is at your disposal to bestow on others'" (p. 85).

of the Most High will overshadow you; and for that reason the holy offspring shall be called the Son of God." (v. 35)

Notice the presence of the Trinity in Jesus' conception. The Holy Spirit will come upon Mary to spark divine life in her human ovum. And the "power of the Most High" will enshroud her, preserving the purity of the embryo and producing the "holy offspring"— the sinless Son of God.

Why did God select such an involved process for Jesus' conception? He had four options at His disposal:

(1) use a good human father and mother, which would result in all humanity but no deity;

(2) create a being, like an angel, with no father or mother, which would be all deity but no humanity;

(3) deposit His spirit into another's body, which would prevent Him from being fully and truly human; or

(4) miraculously conceive a baby within a virgin, which would produce a child fully divine *and* fully human.

Because Jesus' birth is intimately tied to every other aspect of His life, He had to be born of a virgin. The virgin birth is the gate that guards His sinlessness and the door through which God stepped into humanity. Without it, we have no perfect sacrifice, no Savior . . . and, ultimately, no hope.

Mary, however, cannot see through the mists of theology that surround the moment. She just understands that God is planning to do the impossible in *her* body. To further open her mind to God's limitless possibilities, Gabriel goes on to tell her:

> "And behold, even your relative Elizabeth has also conceived a son in her old age; and she who was called barren is now in her sixth month. For nothing will be impossible with God." (vv. 36–37)

With that, Gabriel concludes his message. Mary will bear God's Son, but because she is unwed, the privilege comes with a price: accusations of indecency, pointed fingers, cloaked whispers. Would she be willing to offer herself on the altar of God's plan? Mary has entered her own Gethsemane. Enter with her, and watch her beautiful submission to the Father:

> And Mary said, "Behold, the bondslave of the Lord;
> be it done to me according to your word." And the
> angel departed from her. (v. 38)

Mary and Joseph

In a matter of minutes the encounter is over, and Mary sits alone in stunned silence. But before long, her heart starts bubbling over like a fountain. She is going to have a baby! Her eyes sparkle, her face glows . . . but the words dam up in her throat. Whom can she tell?

Joseph, naturally, is the first person to whom she pours out her secret. Unfortunately, according to Matthew's gospel, he doesn't understand. *What if the rabbis hear about this?* he wonders. *She will be stoned as an adulteress, if not as a blasphemer, for her wild tale about God being the father!*[5] What is he to do with her? He loves her, but how can he marry her?

While Mary hurries to Judea and the refuge of Elizabeth's understanding arms, heartbroken Joseph wrestles with his options. He finally puts the matter to rest with a just but kind plan.

> And Joseph her husband, being a righteous man,
> and not wanting to disgrace her, desired to put her
> away secretly. (Matt. 1:19)

While telling himself he is doing the right thing, Joseph is interrupted by a heavenly visitor—an angel who invades his dreams to confirm Mary's story (vv. 20–21). He, too, obeys God's call and decides that, as soon as Mary returns from Judea, he will marry his precious virgin bride (vv. 24–25).

At this point, it might be helpful to compare Matthew's and Luke's accounts in a chart. The events may have happened in the order of the following chart:

---

5. Sadly, Mary's character has endured many vicious assaults through time. "She has been called in the Talmud the paramour [mistress] of Panthera, a Roman soldier, as Jesus is termed a bastard in the same book. This is the lowest view of Mary, but it is not unlikely that some sharp tongues in Nazareth made her feel the force of this biting slur." Archibald Thomas Robertson, *The Mother of Jesus: Her Problems and Her Glory* (New York, N.Y.: George H. Doran Co., 1925), p. 21. See also John 8:41, in which the Pharisees imply that Jesus was conceived in sin.

Chronology of Significant Events Leading to Jesus' Birth

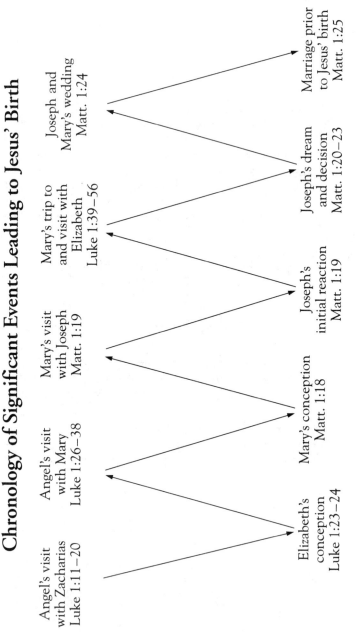

Angel's visit
with Zacharias
Luke 1:11–20

Angel's visit
with Mary
Luke 1:26–38

Mary's visit
with Joseph
Matt. 1:19

Mary's trip to
and visit with
Elizabeth
Luke 1:39–56

Joseph and
Mary's wedding
Matt. 1:24

Marriage prior
to Jesus' birth
Matt. 1:25

Elizabeth's
conception
Luke 1:23–24

Mary's conception
Matt. 1:18

Joseph's
initial reaction
Matt. 1:19

Joseph's dream
and decision
Matt. 1:20–23

Mary and Elizabeth

Meanwhile, miles away from Joseph, Mary has arrived at Elizabeth's house. Elizabeth knows that she herself carries the forerunner, but where is the Christ? The answer is made clear the instant she hears Mary's hello. At the sound of Mary's voice, Elizabeth's baby leaps in her womb, as if to say, "He's here!" Then, filled with the Holy Spirit, Elizabeth exclaims:

> "Blessed among women are you, and blessed is the fruit of your womb! And how has it happened to me, that the mother of my Lord should come to me? For behold, when the sound of your greeting reached my ears, the baby leaped in my womb for joy. And blessed is she who believed that there would be a fulfillment of what had been spoken to her by the Lord." (Luke 1:42b–45)

Mary's response, known as the Magnificat, echoes the feelings of everyone who has tasted from the eternal spring of God's grace. All at once, Mary's pent-up exuberance flows out of her heart in a song rich with scriptural allusions (vv. 46–55).[6]

A Response from Those Who Examine the Evidence

Three months later, Mary returns to Nazareth to wed Joseph (v. 56) and sail into a storm of controversy that would last the rest of her life. But she knows the real story about the wonderful gift God gave her . . . and so do we. Let's draw a couple of applicable truths from her life.

First, *no conception is "ill-timed" to those who realize that God is in full control.* You may have never thought of it this way, but Jesus was the result of an unplanned pregnancy! Perhaps you know someone who is pregnant right now with a baby nobody expected. Take comfort from the fact that God has a plan for that child. No creation of His is ever a mistake.

Second, *such a realization depends on one's perception and submission.* By perception, we mean the way we look at life, from either

---

6. Besides closely resembling Hannah's prayer in 1 Samuel 2:1–10, Mary's hymn of praise parallels several Old Testament passages that Hendricksen lists in his *Exposition of the Gospel according to Luke*, p. 102.

a human or a divine point of view. Mary could have reacted to Gabriel's message from a human perspective: "I can't have a baby now. The timing is all wrong!" But she remained open. When the angel finally unveiled the details, she saw things from God's point of view. She understood and obeyed. That's where *submission* comes into play.

How do you see the events in your life? Do you live in the human, horizontal plane, perhaps objecting because things are out of sync with your timetable? Ask the Lord to help you see things from His point of view. What seems a problem today may turn out to be a gift from the hand of God.

 *Living Insights*

Mary's response to God's working in her life overflows with an enthusiasm that can nourish our own times of worship. Let's divide her hymn of praise—the Magnificat—into four sections, looking at the first two in this study and the last two in our next study. Meditate on each section, then allow her themes to guide your expressions of praise to the Lord.

> "My soul exalts the Lord,
> And my spirit has rejoiced in God my Savior.
> For He has had regard for the humble state of His
>   bondslave;
> For behold, from this time on all generations will
>   count me blessed." (Luke 1:46b–48)

Focus on Mary's name for the Lord, "God my Savior." How have you seen His saving touch in your life? Express your own praise to God *your* Savior, who selected you as His special child.

_____

_____

_____

_____

> "For the Mighty One has done great things for me;
> And holy is His name.

And His mercy is upon generation after generation
Toward those who fear Him." (vv. 49–50)

Draw out God's marvelous attributes from this section. What does it mean to you that He is mighty? Holy? Merciful? Use these thoughts as seedbeds for worship.

_____

_____

_____

_____

Living Insights STUDY TWO

Let's continue worshiping the Lord with Mary's words as inspiration.

"He has done mighty deeds with His arm;
He has scattered those who were proud in the
thoughts of their heart.
He has brought down rulers from their thrones,
And has exalted those who were humble.
He has filled the hungry with good things;
And sent away the rich empty-handed." (vv. 51–53)

Mary was a true princess in God's eyes—not for her bloodline or wealth but for her heart. How have you seen God exalt the Marys of this world? Praise Him for lifting up the poor and the humble and for seeing you as royalty.

_____

_____

_____

_____

"He has given help to Israel His servant,
In remembrance of His mercy,
As He spoke to our fathers,
To Abraham and his offspring forever." (vv. 54–55)

Mary reminds us that God always keeps His promises. Conclude your worship by expressing your faith in Him to fulfill His promises to you in the future.

_____

_____

_____

_____

Digging Deeper

Mary. Catholics revere her as the Queen of Heaven; most Protestants skip over her as a background character in Christ's story. Who is right? And where do our ideas come from? In our quest for a balanced perspective of the one Luke's gospel calls "blessed among women" (1:42), let's examine both positions and evaluate them in the clear light of Scripture.

The Catholic Perspective

Traditional Catholic teaching about Mary revolves around at least four tenets:

1. *Mary as Mediatrix:* This belief asserts that Mary mediates the salvation Christ won for us on the Cross and that none of God's graces come to us except through Mary. This idea takes its roots from Mary's submission to God's will in Luke 1:38, which, to many Catholic theologians since medieval times, means that Christ's incarnation and therefore the redemption of humanity depended on Mary's assent to God's plan. In other words, without Mary agreeing to bear Jesus, we would have no Jesus, no salvation, no grace. Protestants would argue that no human being could stand in the way of God's sovereign will (see 1 Pet. 1:18–21), and that there is only "one mediator also between God and men, the man Christ Jesus" (1 Tim. 2:5).[7]

---

7. Elliot Miller and Kenneth R. Samples, *The Cult of the Virgin: Catholic Mariology and the Apparitions of Mary* (Grand Rapids, Mich.: Baker Book House, 1992), pp. 46–52.

2. *The Immaculate Conception:* This is the belief that Mary herself was conceived without original sin. An older English translation of Gabriel's greeting to Mary in Luke 1:28 is the source for this idea: "Hail, full of grace." This grace, it is believed, was a perfect grace; and being perfect meant that it could not ever have been imperfect, so Mary must have had this perfect grace from the time she was conceived, hence the Immaculate Conception.[8] Protestants would counter this with the frequent scriptural theme contained in Romans 3:23, "For all have sinned and fall short of the glory of God."

3. *Perpetual Virginity:* This is the belief that Mary remained a virgin throughout all of her life. Scriptural basis for this is Mary's question to Gabriel in Luke 1:34, "How can this be, since I am a virgin?" Catholic theologians believe that Mary's words mean she had taken a vow of lifelong celibacy and would *never* know a man. Protestants would take the more literal view of her words and also refer to the mention of Jesus' brothers and sisters in Matthew 13:55–56 and Mark 6:3.[9]

4. *The Assumption:* This is the belief that Mary was taken bodily from earth to heaven so she wouldn't have to endure the corruption of the grave. The line of reasoning goes something like this: "If Mary was conceived without sin, then it would seem reasonable that the result of sin—death—would not be able to hold her, even as it was unable to hold her Son (Acts 2:24)."[10] There is no biblical basis for this; it depends on traditional stories instead. Protestants would dismiss tradition and rely solely on the authority of God's written Word (see Matt. 15:1–9).

The Protestant Response

For fear of venerating Mary, Protestants have tended to go to the opposite extreme and practically ignore her. We are eager to learn from such biblical mothers as Sarah, Isaac's mother; Rachel, Joseph's mother; Jochebed, Moses' mother; Hannah, Samuel's mother; and Elizabeth, John the Baptizer's mother. But when it

---

8. Miller and Samples, *The Cult of the Virgin,* pp. 31–35.

9. Miller and Samples, *The Cult of the Virgin,* pp. 24–29.

10. Miller and Samples, *The Cult of the Virgin,* p. 36.

comes to Mary, who was chosen by God to give life and nurture to Jesus, we back away, in dread of worshiping her.

Neither one of these positions squares with Scripture.

A Scriptural Balance

Are you willing, like Mary, to submit your understanding to God's will and Word (see Luke 1:38)? Then challenge your thinking about this admirable lady—grab hold of a concordance and study for yourself the passages where she is mentioned . . . by God's inspired writers. Learn from her example just as you would from any other Bible character; her life has much to teach us too. She is to be neither exalted nor discounted, but held in esteem as a model of devotion, obedience, and faith.[11]

---

11. Most of our information in this Digging Deeper has been gathered from Elliot Miller and Kenneth R. Samples' fine work *The Cult of the Virgin: Catholic Mariology and the Apparitions of Mary* (Grand Rapids, Mich.: Baker Book House, 1992). The authors examine the beliefs about Mary we've mentioned as well as several more, and they provide a solid Protestant evangelical response. We recommend this book if you would like to study these issues further.

Chapter 5

THE PROPHET OF THE MOST HIGH
Luke 1:57–80

For many people, sundown is the hardest time of the day. For the weary business traveler, the disappearing sun is a reminder of how far away family is. For the working mom, it marks the end of a long day and the beginning of an even longer night. A winter's sundown can numb anybody's spirits with its chilling, ominous shadows.

For Israel, the sun went down when the last prophet, Malachi, slipped beyond the horizon at the close of the Old Testament. Retreating into the night with him were the illuminating rays of God's prophetic presence, and for four hundred years, the nation groped in spiritual darkness.

Anyone could have seen it coming, for the people had long been ignoring the prophets' warnings. And now, having sown the wind, they were reaping the whirlwind (Hos. 8:7).

According to Malachi, their families were falling apart. Husbands were dealing "treacherously" with their wives (2:14), and they had become a nation of "adulterers" and oppressors of "the wage earner . . . the widow and the orphan" (3:5). In a three-pronged indictment against them, the Lord said:

- "You have turned aside from My statutes" (v. 7)

- "You are robbing Me" (v. 9)

- "Your words have been arrogant against Me" (v. 13)

The night dragged on so long that the nation forgot what the sun looked like. Religious hypocrites lit their own puny candles and said, "This is the light." Yet something within the people said, *There must be more.* And, indeed, there was.

The Ancient Prophet Who Promised Another

Malachi told of God's promise that one day the sun would rise and bathe the nation in the brilliance of God's glory:

> "But for you who fear My name the sun of righteousness

will rise with healing in its wings; and you will go
forth and skip about like calves from the stall." (4:2)

From the east, the light from the "sun of righteousness"—the
Messiah—would streak across the land like a golden eagle, dispersing the darkness and bringing "healing in [His] wings." Sin's night
of power would finally be over.

Malachi also prophesied that, before the glorious dawn, a
prophet's voice would sound out, breaking the four-hundred-year
silence:

"Behold, I am going to send you Elijah the prophet
before the coming of the great and terrible day of
the Lord." (v. 5)

This prophet, like Elijah, would be stern, powerful, unintimidated by dignitaries, and undaunted in purpose. And, according to
Malachi, his ministry would touch the people where they needed
it most: in their homes.

"And he will restore the hearts of the fathers to their
children, and the hearts of the children to their fathers,
lest I come and smite the land with a curse." (v. 6)

During the seemingly interminable night, the faithful remnant
in Israel must have read those prophecies again and again for encouragement. As God's remnant today, we learn this important
principle from their example: *When darkness surrounds us, God's
promises keep us hoping.*

Hope is not merely wishing something good will happen. It's
the confidence that God's rope of promises that we're clinging to
will hold fast. God has said that He will "keep in perfect peace"
the one who trusts in Him, and that in Him "we have an everlasting
Rock" (Isa. 26:3–4). As long and dark as the sundown periods of
your life may be, don't lose your grip on God's promises. They're
anchored to the everlasting Rock and are just as reliable.

Elizabeth, the barren wife of the priest Zacharias, clung to the
Lord's promises year after year. Little did she know that, after all
her waiting, He would answer not only her prayers but also the
desperate cries of a darkened world.

The Aging Mother Who Bore the Child

Elizabeth had been infertile as a young woman and was now

40

well past her childbearing years. Her womb was dead—as dead as our hearts under the curse of sin. Yet, marvel of marvels! God enabled her to conceive, and finally, the day arrived for the baby to be born.

> Now the time had come for Elizabeth to give birth, and she brought forth a son. And her neighbors and her relatives heard that the Lord had displayed His great mercy toward her; and they were rejoicing with her. (Luke 1:57–58)

On that wonderful day, God's great mercy took on the form of a tiny baby, yawning and cooing in his mother's arms and peering into his father's loving gaze for the first time.

Has God's mercy been made just as real to you? Has God stirred life within your heart? Has He given you peace in place of fear, freedom instead of bondage? Rejoice! When God sows mercy, praise blossoms in our lives, as it did for this couple and their neighbors and relatives. Their response illustrates a timely principle: *when relief comes, God's mercy helps us rejoice.*

Zacharias rejoiced in a very dramatic way. As you recall, the angel had struck him mute because of his unbelief. For nine long months, Zacharias could only communicate by scribbling notes and gesturing with his hands. Even at his son's birth, his shouts of joy were trapped in silence. Finally, eight days later at the circumcision ceremony, when the boy's name was to be officially announced, God loosed a dam of praise within Zacharias' heart.

The people at the ceremony were going to name the boy Zacharias, after his father. But

> his mother answered and said, "No indeed; but he shall be called John." And they said to her, "There is no one among your relatives who is called by that name." And they made signs to his father,[1] as to what he wanted him called. And he asked for a tablet, and wrote as follows, "His name is John." (vv. 60–63a)

The reading of the name John sent a shock wave of whispers and questions through the crowd, but the buzzing abruptly stopped

---

1. Apparently, the angel struck Zacharias deaf as well as mute, for the people had to communicate to him by sign language.

when a familiar voice rang out. Zacharias was speaking again!

> And they were all astonished. And at once his mouth was opened and his tongue loosed, and he began to speak in praise of God. And fear came on all those living around them; and all these matters were being talked about in all the hill country of Judea. And all who heard them kept them in mind, saying, "What then will this child turn out to be?" For the hand of the Lord was certainly with him. (vv. 63b–66)

Besides the people's reaction, Luke also records the content of Zacharias' praise.

The Once-Silent Father Who Gave God Praise

Zacharias had nine months to think about God's power and his own lack of faith. When he finally got the chance to say something, he used the opportunity to praise the Lord as Elizabeth and Mary had done.

> "Blessed be the Lord God of Israel,
> For He has visited us and accomplished
>   redemption for His people,
> And has raised up a horn of salvation for us
> In the house of David His servant—
> As He spoke by the mouth of His holy prophets
>   from of old—
> Salvation from our enemies,
> And from the hand of all who hate us;
> To show mercy toward our fathers,
> And to remember His holy covenant,
> The oath which He swore to Abraham our father."
> (vv. 68–73)

Right away, he focused on the Lord instead of himself, even though he was the center of attention. He praised the Lord for His plan to redeem Israel and fulfill the covenant He had made with David (see Ps. 89:1–4). Filled with the Holy Spirit, he explained why God was keeping His covenant with the people:

> "To grant us that we, being delivered from the
>   hand of our enemies,

Might serve Him without fear,
In holiness and righteousness before Him all
   our days."
(Luke 1:74–75)

Zacharias' divine discipline had taught him a memorable lesson about serving the Lord without fear; hopefully, Israel had learned the same lesson. Finally, with fatherly pride, Zacharias turned to his infant son and prophesied:

"And you, child, will be called the prophet of
   the Most High;
For you will go on before the Lord to prepare
   His ways;
To give to His people the knowledge of salvation
By the forgiveness of their sins,
Because of the tender mercy of our God,
With which the Sunrise from on high shall visit us,
To shine upon those who sit in darkness and
   the shadow of death,
To guide our feet into the way of peace."
(vv. 76–79)

For four hundred years, discipline's darkness had stifled the nation. But now the Sun was rising! And this nursing newborn would be His prophet.

Any period of discipline, whether in a nation or an individual, can seem never-ending. Yet, as Zacharias models for us, *when discipline ends, God's praise fills our mouths*.

Are you enduring discipline's dark days? Perhaps Zacharias' example can guide you. First, don't press God to end your discipline, but let Him lift the darkness when He's ready. Second, don't hold others responsible for your discipline. And third, when it's time to be restored, draw attention away from yourself and to the Lord and His plan.

The Young Prophet Who Lived in the Desert

The Lord's plan for John required a rugged training ground to build him into a strong man equipped to handle a difficult task. Luke gives us a quick sketch of what John's growing-up years were like:

And the child continued to grow, and to become

strong in spirit, and he lived in the deserts until the
day of his public appearance to Israel. (v. 80)

Already senior citizens when John was born, his parents probably died while he was still a young man. We can imagine him
saying a tearful graveside good-bye, then leaving everything behind
to pursue God's calling in Judea's windswept wilderness. There the
stern, silent hills would become his classroom, and God Himself
would be his tutor. Honed by nature, John would discover a strength
of character in the desert's howling wastelands that he might not
have found anywhere else.

John's solitary training reminds us of a final principle: *when
growth occurs, God's solitude strengthens our souls.* Often our lives
resemble noontime in New York City. The noise, the rush, the
crowds squeezing us from all sides; life's demands towering over us
like skyscrapers, blocking God's guiding light. At those times, we
need to escape the city for the wilderness, where the air is clean,
the landscape is vast, and everything is quiet. There we can hear
God's voice, we can sense His calling . . . and we can see the sunrise.

Living Insights STUDY ONE

Three times, the theme of mercy appears in our passage, like
three cups of cool water offered in love:

- Elizabeth's neighbors and relatives praise the Lord for displaying
  His "great mercy" in her life (Luke 1:58).

- Zacharias says that God kept His covenant with the house of
  David "to show mercy toward our fathers" (v. 72).

- Zacharias prophesies that the "Sunrise from on high shall visit
  us" with "the tender mercy of our God" to bestow salvation and
  forgiveness of sins (v. 78).

God answers the prayer of a barren woman, honors His promise
to a nation, and shines His salvation into a dark world. From one
person to billions, God's mercy reaches every corner of our planet.
Hymn writer Frederick Faber exulted in the breadth of God's mercy:

> There's a wideness in God's mercy
> Like the wideness of the sea;

There's a kindness in His justice
Which is more than liberty.

There is welcome for the sinner
And more graces for the good;
There is mercy with the Savior;
There is healing in His blood.[2]

In what ways has the ocean of God's mercy reached the shores of your life?

An answered prayer: _____

_____

A promise remembered: _____

_____

Forgiveness granted: _____

_____

God's mercy helps us rejoice. In the remaining space, let God's displays of mercy well up in your soul as a fountain of praise. Express to Him your joy for the cups of cool water He has offered you through the years.

_____

_____

_____

_____

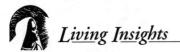 *Living Insights*   STUDY TWO

There's something purifying about the desert. Its starkness makes the sky bluer, the water more precious, the flowers richer, the evenings more refreshing. Things seem clearer, less tangled.

---

2. Frederick W. Faber, "There's a Wideness in God's Mercy," in *The Hymnal for Worship and Celebration* (Waco, Tex.: Word Music, 1986), no. 68.

Unlike a cluttered forest, the desert is vast and free. This is where John the Baptizer met God.

How often our lives resemble a complex forest with our tangled schedules and confining expectations. It is impossible to see very far in the forest; but in the desert, things far away seem so close you could touch them. Could it be that you need some time to retreat to the desert so you can clear your head and reconnect with God?

Even Jesus did this for Himself and the disciples.

> And He said to them, "Come away by yourselves to a lonely place and rest a while." (For there were many people coming and going, and *they did not even have time to eat*.) (Mark 6:31, emphasis added)

Sound like your house? Then, right now, plan a retreat for your spiritual and emotional health. Don't let this thought slip by as a nice but impractical idea. Instead, get creative and brainstorm some ideas on paper. The following questions may help spark your creativity: Where will your place of retreat be? When can you go there? What questions will you ask God? What Scripture will you meditate on?

_____

_____

_____

_____

_____

_____

_____

_____

_____

Experience the desert, and meet God in the lonely places.[3]

---

3. Adapted from the study guide *John the Baptizer*, coauthored by Bryce Klabunde, from the Bible-teaching ministry of Charles R. Swindoll (Anaheim, Calif.: Insight for Living, 1991), pp. 8–9.

Chapter 6

NATIVITY REVISITED

Luke 2:1–20

Gog loves to give us gifts! He delights as we excitedly unwrap His many surprises: an answered prayer, a healing of body or spirit, a new friendship. James tells us that

> every good thing bestowed and every perfect gift is from above, coming down from the Father of lights, with whom there is no variation, or shifting shadow. (1:17)

We may vary or change like the shadows of wind-tossed trees, but His generosity remains constant; even when we turn away from Him, down from heaven comes an endless stream of acceptance and grace. Overwhelmed at God's flood of blessings, Paul once exclaimed: "Thanks be to God for His *indescribable* gift!"[1](2 Cor. 9:15, emphasis added). Other versions and paraphrases have tried to capture Paul's expression in English:

- "unspeakable" (KJV)

- "too wonderful for words" (LB)

- "inexpressible" (RSV)

- "more than we can tell" (BECK)

Certainly, the embodiment of God's greatest gift is Jesus. Who can begin to describe God's tiny present, lovingly wrapped in swaddling clothes on that first Christmas morning? Within Jesus' fragile frame, undiminished deity and true humanity existed together as God's supreme gift of grace to us—a gift too wonderful for words!

A Familiar Setting

We've heard Luke's simple account of Jesus' birth over and over; yet, like a perfect diamond, it never loses its luster nor wears out

---

1. Apparently, Paul had to coin the Greek word *indescribable*, for it appears nowhere else in Greek literature except in later church writings. See Archibald Thomas Robertson, *Word Pictures in the New Testament* (Grand Rapids, Mich.: Baker Book House, 1931), vol. 4, p. 250.

with time. To step into this story is to enter a world of wondrous miracles. God has already placed the divine seed in Mary's virgin womb. Now He plants an idea in Caesar's mind that will begin to turn the giant wheel of world events.

Politically and Geographically

> Now it came about in those days that a decree
> went out from Caesar Augustus, that a census be
> taken of all the inhabited earth. This was the first
> census taken while Quirinius was governor of Syria.
> And all were proceeding to register for the census,
> everyone to his own city. (Luke 2:1–3)

The world packs up and moves at the powerful word of Augustus, who wants to register his subjects for tax purposes. That's what the headlines report, anyway. We know the true story—God is moving the world to deliver a very special package to Bethlehem, the place where the prophet Micah said the Messiah would be born:

> "But as for you, Bethlehem Ephrathah,
> Too little to be among the clans of Judah,
> From you One will go forth for Me to be ruler
>   in Israel.
> His goings forth are from long ago,
> From the days of eternity." (Micah 5:2)

Personally and Individually

Of the sea of citizens who wash out of their villages and pour into their hometowns to register, Luke picks out one travel-weary couple bracing themselves against the current of people swirling around them.

> And Joseph also went up from Galilee, from the city
> of Nazareth, to Judea, to the city of David, which
> is called Bethlehem, because he was of the house
> and family of David, in order to register, along with
> Mary, who was engaged to him,[2] and was with child.
> (Luke 2:4–5)

---

2. Matthew says that Joseph "took [Mary] as his wife" before Jesus' birth (1:24). Luke prefers to think of them as still engaged, probably because, although officially married, they have yet to consummate the union.